Diabetic Recipes for Diabetes type 1:

Over 51 Diabetes Type-1 Quick & Easy Low Cholesterol Whole Foods Recipes

Teresa Moore

Copyright 2018

Your Free Gift

I wanted to show my appreciation that you support my work so I've put together a free gift for you.

Smoothie Recipe Book:
200+ Perfect Smoothies Recipes for Weight Loss Detox, Cleanse and Feel Great in Your Body

Just visit the link above to download it now.

I know you will love this gift.

Thanks!

Table of Contents:

Summer zucchini soup

Cranberry juice

Fried chickpeas

Salad with beans and feta cheese

Pickled cucumbers

Baked tilapia with cheese

Roast Cod

Meatballs in tomato sauce

Vegetable stew in the instant pot

Tomato salad with basil

Florentine cookies

Avocado salad with shrimps

Whole-wheat rye bread

Brussels sprouts in the oven

Cabbage salad with corn and sweet pepper

Carrot soup with dill

Fried green beans with mushrooms and onions

Broccoli with walnuts

Introduction

Dear readers! You all probably know about the existence of such a disease as diabetes. This disease affects many people (both young and old). This book is written mainly for them and their loved ones. Here you will find a lot of useful information. In this book I present to your attention a large number of different recipes that can be used by patients with this serious illness so that the patient has almost the same diverse menu as a healthy person. In addition, here you will learn how you can choose the calorie content you need and learn how to make the right diet.

French ratatouille

Ingredients:

- 1-2 eggplant
- 1-2 zucchini
- 2-3 tomatoes
- 1 onion bulb
- 2 tomatoes
- 1-2 Bulgarian pepper
- 2 cloves of garlic
- salt to taste
- 2-3 tbsp. tablespoons olive oil
- green fresh or dry Provencal herbs

Preparation:

First, we prepare the sauce: shred the onion and fry it, add the wiped tomatoes and chopped Bulgarian peppers into the pan. Stew until the sauce is a bit thick.

Next, cut into circles vegetables and add them alternately in the form, after which we pour the sauce.

Mix olive oil, salt and chopped garlic, pour on the vegetables. Sprinkle with herbs or Provencal herbs, so that it was already completely in French.

Cover the form with foil and send it to the oven. I bake normally at a temperature of 170 gr about 1 hour. You can serve as an independent dish or as a side dish to meat.

Omelets in the instant pot

Ingress:
- 3 eggs
- 3 tablespoons sour cream
- 1 tsp flour
- salt, pepper to taste
- 3 slices of boiled sausage
- 1 tomato
- 1/4 sweet Bulgarian pepper

Preparation:

Eggs beat with a fork, add sour cream, beat again. Add flour, salt, pepper. Mix everything.

Cut tomatoes, sausage, peppers into cubes. Spread evenly on the bottom of the multi-cooker saucepan. Pour the egg mixture.

Put on the Baking mode for 20 minutes.

Chanakhi

Ingress:
- 500 grams of lamb or beef
- 1 onion (finely chopped)
- 500 gr of potatoes
- 3 eggplant
- 2 cloves of garlic
- 3 tablespoons tomato paste
- 2 tomatoes
- 1 Bulgarian pepper
- ½ cup greens (parsley, dill, basil, coriander)

Preparation:
In the pots lay the layers (from the bottom upwards): meat (cubes), onion, potatoes (cubes), eggplant (cubes), garlic (crushed), tomato paste, tomatoes (circles), Bulgarian pepper (finely chopped), greens.

All in a raw state, each layer salt - pepper. A little water (a couple of spoons) to the bottom. Close the lids. Put in a cold oven. At a temperature of 180 ° C, hold for 2 hours.

Green beans with lemon and walnuts

Ingredients:

- 1/2 cup chopped walnuts
- 500 g of green beans, trim the ends and cut into pieces 4 cm long
- 30 g butter, melt
- 1 lemon, squeeze juice and remove the zest
- salt and pepper to taste

Preparation:

Preheat the oven to 190 C. Lay the nuts in one layer on a baking sheet. Fry in a preheated oven until the nuts are lightly browned, about 5 to 10 minutes. Put the string beans in a steamer over a 3 cm layer of water and cover. Cook for a couple of 8 - 10 minutes, or until the bean is soft, but retains a bright green color. Put the boiled beans in a large bowl and mix with butter, lemon juice and lemon zest. Season with salt and pepper. Transfer the beans to a dish and sprinkle with toasted nuts. Immediately serve on the table.

Couple steaks

Ingredients:

- 2 slices of bread
- 400-500 g minced meat
- 1 cup of milk or cream (250 ml)
- 1 egg white
- salt, pepper, spices to taste

Preparation:

Bread soak in water and squeeze when it swells.

Minced meat and milk mixer or in a blender at low speed.

Separately whisk the protein to foam (use a clean dry bowl and clean dry blades for the mixer).

Gently add minced whipped protein, soaked bread, salt and spices to taste. Stir gently.

Slap the cutlets, put them in a steamer or in a steam basket in an instant pot and cook for a couple of 25 minutes.

Salad from buckwheat and lentils

Ingredients:

- 1 liter of vegetable broth
- 1 glass of green or brown lentils, rinse and drain the water
- 2 tablespoons vegetable oil
- 2 onions
- 2 stalks of celery
- 3 carrots, cut
- 2 cloves of garlic
- 2 tablespoons Provençal herbs or any other seasoning
- 1/4 tsp. dry oregano or marjoram
- 1/4 tsp. dry thyme
- 1 tsp ground cumin (zira)
- a pinch of red ground pepper (to taste)
- 1 egg (optional)
- 1 cup buckwheat
- 1 tbsp. vegetable oil
- 1/2 tsp. salt
- 1 tbsp. vinegar

Preparation6

Boil broth, pour lentils, reduce heat and simmer for 15-20 minutes. Drain the broth in a separate bowl (it is still useful). Put the lentils in a salad bowl.
In the frying pan, heat the vegetable oil, fry the chopped onion, stirring. Add celery, carrots and garlic and continue cooking until softened carrots, another 10 minutes. Transfer vegetable toast in lentils. Add seasoning, stir.
Beat in egg bowl. Mix with buckwheat. Heat a spoon in the pan and add the buckwheat with the egg. Cook over medium heat, stirring, for 10 minutes. Pour 2 cups of broth, bring to a boil. Reduce heat and cook until liquid is absorbed and buckwheat is ready, 20-25 minutes.
Mix buckwheat with lentils. Salt and pepper. Add a spoonful of oil and vinegar. (To the taste). Mix. Serve the salad warm or chilled.

Beef in the oven

Ingredients:
- 2 tsp. olive oil
- 1 (2kg) beef (neck / shoulder blade)
- 1 onion, finely chopped
- 2 cloves garlic, chop
- 2 bay leaves
- Salt and freshly ground black pepper to taste

Preparation:
Preheat the oven to 160 ° C.
Heat a heavy frying pan over medium heat. Add butter and fry the meat on all sides, about 10 minutes.
Lay the onions, garlic and 1 bay leaf on the bottom of a heavy pan or baking dish. Top with meat, remaining bay leaf, salt-pepper and cover with a lid or foil.
Bake in the oven for about 30 minutes. Reduce heat to 150 ° C and bake 1 1/2 hours. Put the meat on the dish, cover with foil and let stand for 10 - 15 minutes.
Slice into slices, top with onion and pour over the juice.

Green beans with garlic in the oven

Ingredients:

- 1 kg of green beans
- 1 large onion
- 8 cloves of garlic
- 2 tablespoons olive oil
- salt and pepper to taste
- 2 tablespoons wine or balsamic vinegar

Preparation:

Lubricate the baking sheet with vegetable oil. Lay the beans. Cut the onions into large rings, lay them on the beans. Chop garlic into halves. Spread over the beans. Pour vegetables 2 tbsp. olive oil, salt-pepper.
Bake without covering at 200 C for about 30 minutes. Open and stir every 10 minutes, after 20 minutes, check periodically for readiness.
Ready beans drizzle with vinegar.

Cupcakes from cottage cheese "With a drop of love"

Ingredients:
- 2 chicken eggs
- 400 g cottage cheese
- 6 tbsp. spoons of sugar
- 4 tbsp. tablespoons semolina
- 4 tbsp. spoons of flour
- 1 teaspoon of soda, slaked vinegar

Preparation:
First, beat the egg and sugar in a bowl until the foam turns out.

Then add the cottage cheese to the egg mass, mix thoroughly, so that the mass becomes almost homogeneous.

Pour into the bowl of flour, semolina, soda, which previously extinguished with vinegar, and a pinch of vanillin.

We take 5 medium molds and we grease them with vegetable oil, so that our cupcakes do not burn.

Fill molds with a dough and put in a preheated oven for 30 minutes.

Serve cupcakes better cooled, if desired, you can sprinkle them with powdered sugar or coconut chips to decorate their ruddy crust.

Appetizer of tomatoes with Parmesan cheese

Ingredients:

- 200 g of cheese
- 2 boiled eggs
- 2 cloves of garlic
- 1 bunch of parsley
- 4 large tomatoes
- salt pepper
- 3 tablespoons mayonnaise

Preparation:

Prepare a cheese salad. To do this: grate cheese, eggs. Squeeze out the garlic and finely chop the parsley.

Mix cheese, greens, garlic and eggs. All salt and pepper to taste. Add the mayonnaise and mix well.

Cut the tomatoes in circles. Put on a plate, on top put on each slice of tomato cheese salad (1 tsp).

Stewed zucchini or eggplant

Ingredients:

- 1 onion finely chopped
- 3 carrots finely chopped
- 2-3 tomatoes, finely chopped
- 500 grams of zucchini, peeled, cut into small cubes
- 2 cloves garlic, finely chopped
- 1/4 cup chopped parsley
- 2 tablespoons tomato paste (or to taste)
- 1 tsp salt (or to taste)
- 1/4 tsp. ground pepper

Preparation:

Put out the onion, garlic, and carrots in vegetable oil - 5 minutes. Stir, do not let burn, stew on medium heat. Add the tomatoes, simmer for another 5 minutes, stirring. Add zucchini or eggplants, peeled and cut into small cubes, stew for 5 minutes. Salt, pepper, add 2 tablespoons. tomato paste. Stir, close the lid and simmer for another 10 minutes on low heat.
In the end add parsley.

Baked Eggplants with Tomatoes

Ingredients:

- 1 eggplant, cut into slices 1.5 cm thick
- 1 tomato, cut into slices
- 1/4 cup grated hard cheese

Preparation:

Preheat the oven to 200 ° C.

Lubricate the pan with oil. Lay the eggplant slices on a baking tray, sprinkle with grated cheese on top. Over the cheese for each eggplant circle lay out a circle of tomato. Sprinkle cheese again. If the cheese has a softer taste than Parmesan, you can additionally salt and pepper.

Bake for 10-15 minutes in a preheated oven.

Vegetables in the oven

Ingredients:
- 400 g pumpkin or winter squash
- 2 red sweet peppers, remove the seeds and cut into squares
- 1 sweet potato (sweet potato), peeled and cut into cubes
- 3 yellow potatoes, cut into cubes
- 1 red onion, cut into quarters (large feathers)
- 1 tbsp. chopped fresh thyme or dry
- 2 tablespoons chopped fresh rosemary
- 1/4 cup olive oil
- 2 tablespoons wine or balsamic vinegar (or lemon juice)
- Salt and ground black pepper to taste

Preparation:
Preheat the oven to 250 ° C.
In a large bowl, mix the winter zucchini, red bell pepper, sweet potato and yellow potatoes. Divide the red onions into quarters and add to the vegetables.
In a small bowl, mix thyme, rosemary, olive oil, vinegar, salt and pepper. Mix with the vegetables until they are evenly coated with this mixture. Evenly put in a large baking dish.
Bake for 35 to 40 minutes in a preheated oven (250C),
stirring every 10 minutes, or until the vegetables are ready and browned.

Salmon in the oven with garlic and dill

Ingredients:

- 1.5 kg salmon fillets (with skin)
- 1 head of garlic, peel
- 30 g fresh dill, finely chopped
- 50 ml of olive oil
- 1 tsp salt and pepper, or to taste

Preparation:

In a blender or combine, skip the garlic, add dill and olive oil and give another couple of turns.

Wash the fillets and dry. Put in a baking dish or on a baking sheet down. Pre-grease the pan with oil. Put the garlic mass over the fish and take the marinade in the refrigerator for 2 hours.

Preheat the oven to 190C.

Bake in a preheated oven for 15 minutes. Do not overdo it, otherwise the fish will be dry. The fish is ready when the flesh can be divided into pieces by a fork.

Oatmeal cocktail

Ingredients:
- 1 cup soy milk
- 1/2 cup of oatmeal
- 1 banana
- 1 cup frozen strawberries
- 1/2 tsp. vanilla
- 1 1/2 tsp. sugar (optional)

Preparation:
Add soy milk, oats, banana and berries to the blender. Add vanilla and sugar, if you want. Grind until smooth. Pour into glasses.

Buckwheat with chicken in tomato sauce

Ingredients:

- 1 cup of buckwheat
- 2 cups of water
- 350 g chicken breasts
- 3 tablespoons butter
- 1 onion
- 1 cup tomato sauce
- 1 bay leaves
- salt and pepper to taste

Preparation:

Boil buckwheat: A glass of buckwheat pour 2 glasses of water, and cook without mixing on medium heat, until the water is completely absorbed and the croup will not become soft.

Chicken breast is slightly discouraged and cut into thin strips.

In butter, fry the finely chopped onion until it is clear, about 5 minutes.

Add the chicken to the onion, stir-fry for about 5 minutes. Salt and pepper.

Pour the tomato sauce, add bay leaf, salt, pepper and simmer for 5-7 minutes.

Ready to put on buckwheat butter. Spread on plates, lay on top of chicken, pour with sauce.

Lentil soup in Greek

Ingredients:
- 200 g of brown lentils
- 60 ml of olive oil (4 tbsp.)
- 1 tbsp. chopped garlic
- 1 onion, finely chopped
- 1 large carrot, finely chopped
- 1 liter of water
- 1 pinch of dried oregano
- 1 pinch of ground dried rosemary (optional)
- 2 bay leaves
- 1 tbsp. tomato paste
- 1 pinch of salt and pepper to taste
- 1 tsp wine vinegar (or to taste)
- 1 tsp olive oil (or to taste)

Preparation:
Lentils should be filled with water in a large saucepan (the water level should be about 3 cm above the lentils). Put on medium fire. After boiling, cook for 10 minutes, after which throw the lentils on a strainer.

Dissolve the pan, pour olive oil and put on medium heat. Add the garlic, onions and carrots. Stew, stirring, until the onion is soft and translucent, about 5 minutes. Add welded lentils, 1 liter of water, oregano, rosemary and bay leaf. Boil. Reduce heat, cover, cook for 10 minutes.

Add the tomato paste, salt, pepper to taste. Cover and cook until the lentils are ready, 30 to 40 minutes, stirring occasionally. If the soup is too thick, dilute with water.

Herculean porridge in the instant pot

Ingredients:

- 2 glasses of oatmeal
- 4 glasses of water
- 1/2 tsp. salt

Preparation:

In the evening, fill in the instant pot Hercules, water, salt. You can mix it lightly. I sometimes add a spoonful of yogurt or natural yogurt (for better digestion). I turn on the porridge mode, the delay timer (put at 6:30 am) and go to sleep! If you bet in the morning - put on porridge
At 6:30 the porridge is ready!
Variants for cereal (when bored) - butter, yogurt, jam, frozen fruit (especially if hot and you must quickly cool), granulated sugar, cinnamon, honey, flaxseed ground, condensed milk, coconut chips, grated apples, etc.

Bean and corn salad

Ingredients:
- 1 lime
- 1/2 cup olive oil
- 1 clove of garlic
- 1 tsp salt
- 1/8 tsp. cayenne pepper (red ground pepper)
- 2 400 g cans of beans, rinse and recline
- 1 1/2 cups (250 g) of frozen corn
- 1 avocado
- 1 sweet red pepper, chopped
- 2 tomatoes, chopped
- 6 stalks of green onion
- 1/2 cup chopped cilantro (optional)

Preparation:
Combine the juice of lime, olive oil, garlic, salt and cayenne pepper in a small jar. Cover and shake vigorously until the ingredients are well mixed.
In a salad bowl, mix beans, corn, avocado (cut into cubes), sweet peppers, tomatoes, onions and coriander. Shake the dressing again and pour a salad on it. Stir and serve.

Stuffed peppers in the instant pot

Ingredients:

- 6 medium sized Bulgarian peppers
- 200g minced meat
- 5 tablespoons rice
- 1 onion
- 4 tomatoes
- salt, pepper to taste
- greenery
- 2-3 tablespoons vegetable oil
- 200-250 ml of vegetable broth

Preparation:

Boil rice until half cooked in a small amount of water, adding a little salt.

Finely chop onion and fry in vegetable oil.

Tomatoes scalded with boiling water, peeled the skin and put out with onions 5-10 minutes.

Mix the minced meat, rice and stewed vegetables. Add salt, pepper, greens and mix thoroughly.

Remove the peppers from seeds, rinse and fill with filling.

Put the peppers in a saucepan of instant pot and pour the broth. Cook in the 'Quenching" 1 hour.

Onion finely chopped, fry in vegetable oil until golden brown. Add small pieces of chicken fillet (1.5-2 cm) and chopped carrots, fry for 5 minutes.

At this time, wash the rice and add to the chicken (no water). Close the lid and put out 10-15 minutes. From time to time stir.

Zucchini cut into large strips or small cubes, add to rice with chicken and simmer under the lid for 10-15 minutes or until the rice is ready, stirring.

At the end add lecho or tomato sauce. You can dilute 2-3 tablespoons water. tomato paste. If you take fresh tomatoes, then put them together with zucchini.

Cabbage rolls

Ingredients:

- 1 head of cabbage
- 500 g ground beef
- 300 g of minced pork
- 3/4 cup of rice
- 2 onions
- salt pepper
- 3 small carrots
- 2-3 tablespoons vegetable oil
- 2 tablespoons tomato sauce (or ketchup)
- 2 tablespoons sour cream

Preparation:

In cabbage make an incision around the stump, or immediately cut out a stump. Put the cabbage into the boiling water. Cook for about 15-20 minutes.

Head to the leaves. In large leaves, cut thickenings at the base of the leaf.

Boil rice for about 10 minutes. One onion cut and fry in vegetable oil until transparent.

Mix the pork and ground beef, add the fried onions and rice. Salt and season with pepper the resulting mass, mix everything well.

On the base of the cabbage leaf, put the filling (about 1 tablespoon) with an envelope.

The resulting cabbage rolls fry in vegetable oil for several minutes on each side. Transfer the cabbage rolls into a saucepan or saucepan. Top with a grated carrot, finely chopped onion. Salt lightly.

Mix sour cream and ketchup and about a glass of water, add salt, pepper or your favorite seasonings. Pour the cabbage rolls with the resulting sauce.

Cover and stew for 45 minutes.

Light mushroom soup

Ingredients:

- 1 medium onion, finely chopped
- 1 carrot, finely chopped
- 1,5 - 2 cups of finely chopped mushrooms
- 1.5 liters of water
- salt, pepper to taste
- 1 mushroom bouillon cube (optional)
- 2 potatoes
- 1/3 cup small pasta
- chopped dill
- sour cream

Preparation:

Fry the onion and carrots in butter for 5-7 minutes, add chopped mushrooms and put out the minutes 5.
Boil 1.5 liters of water, add salt to taste. If desired, you can add 1 mushroom bouillon cube. Put 2 finely chopped potatoes, add browned vegetables and mushrooms. Cook for 5 minutes. Add 1/3 cup of small pasta, cook for another 5 minutes. Pepper, add chopped dill.
Serve with sour cream.

Squash pancakes in the oven

Ingredients:
- 1 medium zucchini
- 1 small carrot
- 1 small onion
- 3 sprigs of dill
- 1 egg
- 2-3 tablespoons flour
- 120 g of crumbled cheese or cottage cheese

For sauce:
- 100 g unsweetened yogurt or sour cream
- 1 clove of garlic
- 2 tablespoons olive oil
- salt and pepper to taste

Preparation:
Grate zucchini on a grater on a clean kitchen towel and sprinkle with salt. Wait 10 minutes, and then squeeze the juice.

In the meantime, grate the carrots and chop finely the onion, chop the dill. In a large bowl, mix the vegetables, dill, add a lightly beaten egg. The dough should not be liquid. Add flour and cheese or cottage cheese. Very tasty is obtained with soft goat cheese.

Preheat the oven to 180 ° C. Cover the baking sheet with baking paper and grease with vegetable oil. Spread a tablespoon on a pancake pan, about the same size, leaving a space between the fritters. Bake 20-25 minutes until golden brown.

For the sauce, mix the yogurt or sour cream with the garlic passed through the press. Add salt, pepper. Add dill if desired. Hot pancakes served with garlic sauce.

Delicate radish salad radish and carrots

Ingredients:
- 1 radish daikon
- 2 carrots
- 1 green apple
- 3-4 stalks of celery (optional)
- 1/2 cup raisins
- 3 tbsp. olive oil
- 2 tablespoons lemon juice
- slightly chopped parsley
- 1 clove of garlic
- salt and pepper

Preparation:
Grate radish daikon. On a large grater, grate the carrot. Apple cut into strips.
Celery cut into thin slices.
Mix the vegetables. Add raisins and finely chopped parsley.
Lemon juice mixed with olive oil and squeezed garlic.
Season the salad, mix well.

Red fish baked in foil

Ingredients:
- 1 kg of red fish (salmon, salmon)
- salt
- seasoning for fish
- 3 tablespoons olive oil
- 2 cloves of garlic
- 2 tablespoons soy sauce
- 1 tsp shredded ginger
- 1 tbsp. honey (optional)
- lemon peel
- some fresh parsley

Preparation:
Fish gutted and washed, cut in half. Remove the spinal bone, small pips it is convenient to take out with tweezers: draw a palm where there is a stitch - stick a bone, just pull it out with tweezers. Season the red fish and sprinkle with the seasoning for the fish.

Olive oil mixed with sliced garlic, soy sauce, ginger, grated zest and honey. With the resulting marinade, grease the fish and sprinkle with chopped parsley.

Lay a foil leaf on the baking tray with a stock, so that you can wrap the fish. Lubricate the foil lightly with vegetable oil and lay the red fish skin down. Turn the fish into foil, lifting the edges. Put the baking tray with fish in the oven, preheated to 200 C. Bake for about 20 minutes, then open the foil and bake for another 10-15 minutes to get the top browned.

Children's cottage cheese casserole

Ingress:

- 4 tablespoons sour cream
- 2 tablespoons semolina
- 400 g cottage cheese
- 2 eggs
- 3-4 tablespoons sugar
- a pinch of salt
- oil for lubrication of molds

Preparation:

Munch the mixture with sour cream, leave for 30 minutes, so that the mango is soaked.

Cottage cheese beat with eggs and sugar. Add salt, sugar, mix well. Then add the swollen mango with sour cream.

Shape the oil with oil, lay out the curd mass, smooth. Put the oven in a preheated oven. Bake for about 40 minutes.

Salad from spinach and radishes

Ingredients:
- 400 g fresh spinach (better young)
- 150 grams of radish
- 1/3 cup vegetable oil
- 1 lemon (squeeze out the juice)
- 1 tsp mustard
- 1 clove of garlic, chop
- salt and pepper to taste

Preparation:
Spinach leaves are better to tear into several pieces, rather than cut with a knife. So spinach will remain fresh and will not wither in a salad. Cut the radish into thin slices.

Mix the ingredients for refilling in the jar with the lid. Close the lid and shake well to obtain a uniform mass. Serve the salad immediately before serving.

Salmon in foil

Ingredients:

- 700 g of salmon fillets
- salt and pepper to taste
- 3 cloves garlic, crush
- 1 sprig of fresh dill, finely chopped
- 5 slices of lemon
- 5 sprigs of fresh dill
- 2 tuft of onion, finely chopped

Preparation:

Preheat the oven to 230C. Lubricate two large sheets of foil.
Place the salmon fillet on the foil sheet. Sprinkle with salt, pepper, garlic and chopped dill. From the top, spread slices of lemon, for each slice - a sprig of fresh dill. Sprinkle onions with green onions.
Cover the salmon with a second sheet of foil and tighten and tuck the edges well.
Place on a baking tray or in a mold.
Bake in a preheated oven for 20-25 minutes, until the salmon is easily separated by a fork.

Dietary salad from cabbage and beets

Ingredients:

- 200 g cabbage, shuffle thinner
- 1 small raw beet, grate
- 1/2 apple, grate
- 2 cloves of garlic
- juice of half a lemon or 1 tbsp. 9% vinegar
- 1/2 tsp. salt or taste
- 1/2 tsp. sugar or to taste
- 2 tablespoons chopped parsley

Preparation:

Shred cabbage thinner. Add 1/2 tsp. salt and rubbed with hands.
Add grated beets, crushed garlic, grated apple, lemon juice (or vinegar), sugar. Mix everything and let stand for 15 minutes.
Sprinkle with chopped parsley.

Dietary salad from cabbage and beets

- 200 g cabbage, shuffle thinner
- 1 small raw beet, grate
- 1/2 apple, grate
- 2 cloves of garlic
- juice of half a lemon or 1 tbsp. 9% vinegar
- 1/2 tsp. salt or taste
- 1/2 tsp. sugar or to taste
- 2 tablespoons chopped parsley

Preparation:

Shred cabbage thinner. Add 1/2 tsp. salt and rubbed with hands.
Add grated beets, crushed garlic, grated apple, lemon juice (or vinegar), sugar. Mix everything and let stand for 15 minutes.
Sprinkle with chopped parsley.

Soup made of lentils

Ingredients:

- 1.5 cups of lentils
- 3 liters of water
- 300 g semi-smoked sausage or ham
- 1 stick of celery, finely chopped
- 1 onion, finely chopped
- 2 carrots, cut
- 2 potatoes, cut into cubes
- 1/4 tsp. pepper
- 2 cloves of garlic
- 3 tablespoons tomato paste
- 2 tsp. salt
- parsley for serving

Preparation:

In a frying pan on medium heat, toss the onions until softening, add garlic, carrots, celery and tomato paste and put out all the minutes. 10.

Rinse the lentils, add water, vegetables from the frying pan and other ingredients. Cook over low heat for about 1 hour, stirring occasionally until the lentils are boiled. Salt and pepper to taste.

Broccoli with tomatoes and basil

Ingredients:

- 2 tablespoons olive oil
- 2 cloves garlic, chop
- 1 (400 g) a can of tomatoes in its own juice, cut into
- 1 tsp wine vinegar
- 1/4 cup chopped fresh basil or 1 tbsp. dry
- 500 grams of broccoli
- Salt and ground black pepper to taste

Preparation:

Heat the olive oil in a large frying pan over medium heat. Add the garlic and stifle, stirring constantly. Add the tomatoes, basil and vinegar and cook until the liquid evaporates about half.

Put the broccoli over the tomatoes and season with a little salt and pepper. Stew on low heat for 10 minutes, or until the broccoli is tender. Do not overcook the broccoli, it should remain bright green. Place in a serving dish and mix with sauce before serving.

Summer zucchini soup

Ingredients:
- 2 tablespoons vegetable oil
- 1 onion
- 2 cloves of garlic
- 1 carrot
- 1 zucchini (500-700g)
- 1 tsp curry seasoning
- salt and pepper to taste
- 1 liter of broth or water
- 50 g of melted or grated hard cheese

Additionally:
- 100 grams of ham or sausage
- handful of chopped greens

Preparation:
In a saucepan in vegetable oil fry the chopped onions and garlic to lightly browned. Add grated carrots, put out for a few minutes. Add a large chopped zucchini, 1 glass of water or broth, and leave to simmer under the lid for 20 minutes, until the zucchini is ready.

Add 1 tsp. seasoning curry, salt and pepper to taste. Pour another glass of water or broth, bring to a boil. Remove from heat and turn the soup directly in a saucepan with a submerged blender, until smooth.

Add grated cheese, and another 1-2 cups of water or broth (to the desired density). Spread soup on plates, add a handful of sliced ham or sausage, sprinkle with chopped greens.

Cranberry juice

Ingredients:

- 1 cup of cranberry
- 1 liter of water
- 1 tbsp. Honey

Preparation:

Cranberry mash with a wooden spoon. Squeeze the juice, skins pour 1 liter of cold water and boil.
Decoction slightly cool. Add 1 tablespoon of honey and mix with the juice.

Fried chickpeas

Ingredients:

- 400 g of chick pea (pea), drain the liquid
- 2 tablespoons olive oil
- 1 pinch of salt
- 1 pinch of garlic seasoning
- 1 pinch of cayenne or red ground pepper

Preparation:

Preheat the oven to 230 ° C.

Pease peas with paper or clean kitchen towels. In a bowl, mix the peas with olive oil and season to taste with salt, garlic seasoning and red pepper (if desired). Spread evenly on a baking sheet and bake for 30-40 minutes until the peas are browned and crunchy. Closely monitor the last few minutes to prevent peas from burning.

Salad with beans and feta cheese

Ingredients:

- 400 g can of canned beans
- 150 g of brynza
- 150 g of salad greens
- 1/2 cup olives
- parsley dill
- salt pepper
- 2 tablespoons vegetable oil
- 1 tbsp. wine or balsamic vinegar
- 1 clove of garlic

Preparation:

With the beans drained of liquid, rinse under cold water.
Brynza cut into cubes. In a salad bowl put greens, olives, add cheese and beans.
Finely chop the dill and parsley and add to the salad. Salt and season with pepper.

Pickled cucumbers

Ingredients:

- 1 kg of cucumbers
- leaves of black currant, horseradish, dill
- 3-4 cloves garlic, coarsely chopped
- 1 liter of water
- 2 tablespoons salt

Preparation:

Cucumbers to wash, put in a bowl, lay with washed greens and garlic.
Boil water, dissolve in water 2 tbsp. salt. Pour the brine cucumber. Press the lid or the plate so that the cucumbers remain completely immersed in the brine.
Leave for at least 6 hours.

Baked tilapia with cheese

Ingredients:

- 1 kg fillet of tilapia
- 0.5 cups of grated Parmesan cheese
- 50 g of softened butter
- 3 tablespoons mayonnaise
- 2 tablespoons lemon juice
- 1/4 tsp. dry garlic
- 1/4 tsp. ground black pepper
- 1/4 tsp. dry basil (or other seasoning to taste)

Preparation:

Turn on the oven grill (the upper heating element, it is not in all the ovens there, unfortunately). Lubricate the pan with oil.

In a bowl, combine Parmesan cheese, butter, and mayonnaise and lemon juice. Add seasonings and spices. Stir.

Lay the fish on a baking sheet in one layer. Place the pan at the top of the oven, just under the heating element (at a distance of 5-10 cm). Bake 2-3 minutes, turn over and bake for 2-3 more minutes on the other side. Take the baking tray out of the oven and put the cheese mixture on the fish. Bake for 2 more minutes or until the top turns brown, and the fish begins to separate into pieces with a fork. Do not overdo the fish - it will be dry.

Roast Cod

Ingredients:

- 4 cod fillets of 150 grams each
- 1 red sweet pepper
- 2 tomatoes
- 1 onion
- 1 clove of garlic
- 2 tablespoons of the basil
- 2 tablespoons olive oil
- juice of 1 lemon
- salt and pepper

Preparation:

Preheat the oven to 200 degrees.

Pepper and tomatoes cut into cubes. Mix with finely chopped onion, garlic and basil. Add the olive oil.

Prepare 4 sheets of foil. On each sheet lay a piece of fish, and on top of the vegetable mixture, sprinkle with lemon juice, salt and pepper. Top with foil, making an envelope.

Put in the oven for 20 minutes.

Meatballs in tomato sauce

Ingredients:

- 1 slice of white bread
- 50 ml of milk
- 500 g turkey stuffing
- bunch of fresh parsley
- 200 grams of frozen spinach
- salt and pepper to taste
- 1/4 cup olive oil
- 1 onion
- 2 cloves of garlic
- 1 carrot
- 300 grams of tomato sauce

Preparation:

A slice of bread soak in the milk. Minced meat mixed with soaked bread, add chopped parsley, thawed spinach, salt and pepper. Form small cutlets.
In olive oil (2 tablespoons) fry the cutlets for 3 minutes, remove and set them aside.
Top up the remaining oil, fry onion and garlic. Add the finely chopped carrots.
Pour the tomato sauce, let it boil and stew the meatballs for 15-20 minutes.
Serve with pasta or rice.

Vegetable stew in the instant pot

Ingredients:

- 1 medium rutabaga or turnip
- 2 potatoes
- 3-4 carrots
- 0.5 small head of cabbage, chop
- 0.5 cans of green peas
- 1 tsp salt

Preparation:

Pryukva or turnip cubes. Also we cut carrots and potatoes.

If you have turnips - then put it in a instant pot with a little water and turn on steam for steam for 10 minutes. As soon as it boils, drain the water. This is done so that the turnip does not bitter. I had a sweet rye bread, I threw it along with all the other vegetables.

Fold all vegetables in a instant pot (except for canned peas). My instant pot was crammed under the cover. Turn on the Quenching mode for 30 minutes.

After 30 minutes, add the peas, mix well. To try cabbage for readiness. You may need to turn it on for another 15 minutes.

In the end, along with peas, you can also add roasted sliced sausages.

Tomato salad with basil

Ingredients:

- 4 ripe tomatoes, coarsely chopped
- 1/2 cup freshly sliced basil leaves
- 1/2 tsp. salt
- 1/4 tsp. black ground pepper
- 1 tbsp. wine vinegar
- 3 tablespoons olive oil
- 2 cloves of garlic, squeeze through garlic

Preparation:

Mix everything. Leave to stand for 10 minutes.

Florentine cookies

Ingredients:

- 50 g of butter
- 50 g (4 tablespoons) of sugar
- 2 tablespoons milk
- 25 g (1/4 cup) of pumpkin seeds
- 40 g (1/4 cup) of pine nuts
- 50 grams (1/2 cup) of raisins
- 50 grams (1/4 cup) of dried cranberries or cherries
- 2 tablespoons flour

Preparation:

Melt the butter in a small saucepan and add sugar to it. Heat until bubbles appear on the surface.

Remove the saucepan from the plate, pour in 2 tablespoons of milk, add seeds, nuts, raisins and cranberries. Pour in the flour. All mix well.

Preheat the oven to 180 degrees. Cover the parchment with parchment paper and lay out the cookies with a teaspoon.

Bake for 10 minutes until the cookie turns golden.

Avocado salad with shrimps

Ingredients:

- 3 mature avocados
- 2 tablespoons lemon juice
- 150 gr of shrimps
- 2 tablespoons dill
- 1 celery stick
- 1 clove of garlic
- 2 tablespoons mayonnaise
- salt and white ground pepper to taste

Preparation:

Avocado cut in half. Remove the stone and the flesh with a spoon, keeping the peel.
Cut the avocado into cubes, pour lemon juice so that the avocado does not darken.
Boil the shrimp. If they are large-cut. You can use small cocktail shrimp.
Finely chop dill, celery as thin as possible. Rub or squeeze out the garlic.
Shrimp, celery, garlic, dill mixed with avocado. Season with mayonnaise. Add salt and pepper to taste.
Put in the cups from the rind.

Whole-wheat rye bread

Ingredients:

- 2 glasses of whole meal rye flour
- 3/4 glasses of water at room temperature
- 2 tablespoons sugar (or sweetener)
- 1 tsp salt (can be reduced to 1/2 tsp)
- 1 tsp dry yeast.
- 1 + 1/2 tablespoons. vegetable oil

Preparation:

Download all the ingredients in the bread maker.
Enable the mode for whole grain bread.
After the completion of the regime, transfer the bread to the grate for the oven and allow it to cool slightly.

Brussels sprouts in the oven

Ingredients:

- 500 g Brussels sprouts, ends trim and remove yellow leaves
- 3 tablespoons olive oil
- 1 tsp salt
- 1/2 tsp. freshly ground black pepper

Preparation:

Preheat the oven to 200 ° C.

Depending on the size, you can bake entire rounds, or cut in half or quarter. In a bowl, mix the cabbage with olive oil, salt and pepper. Put on a baking sheet and put on a medium grate in the oven.

Bake for 30 to 45 minutes, shaking the baking tray every 5 to 7 minutes to make the cabbage uniformly brown. If necessary, lower the fire to prevent the cabbage from burning. Ready-baked Brussels sprouts should be dark brown.

Cabbage salad with corn and sweet pepper

Ingredients:

- 1 small head of cabbage, chopped (about 4 glasses)
- 1 sweet pepper, chopped
- 1 cup finely chopped green onions
- 1 cup corn (fluid drained)
- 4 tablespoons Table vinegar 9% (or 0.5 cups 5%)
- 3 tablespoons sugar (or sugar substitute)
- salt and pepper to taste
- 1 tsp finely chopped chili pepper (optional)
- 0.5 cup chopped cilantro (optional)

Preparation:

Stir all the ingredients. Cabbage does not need to be reaped.

Carrot soup with dill

Ingredients:

- 500 g carrots, sliced
- 2 tsp. vegetable oil
- 2 tsp. chopped garlic
- 1 cup of onion, finely chopped
- 3 1/2 glasses of chicken broth
- 3/4 cup of milk
- 2 tablespoons chopped fresh dill
- 2 tablespoons chopped fresh onion

Preparation:

Bring a large pot of water to a boil. Add the carrots and cook until done, not longer. Drain the water and return the carrots to a saucepan. Set it aside.
Heat the vegetable oil in a frying pan over medium heat. Quench the onions and garlic until soft, about 5 minutes. Transfer the onion and garlic into a pot of carrots and pour in the chicken broth. Reduce heat to medium low, cover with a lid and cook for 25 minutes to mix the flavors.
Grind the carrot mixture in a food processor or blender, in small portions, if necessary. Return to a pan and add milk, dill and green onions. Cook until the soup warms up, but no more and serve.

Fried green beans with mushrooms and onions

Ingredients:
- 800 g of string beans
- 200 g of champignon
- 1-2 onions
- butter or vegetable oil for frying
- 2 cloves of garlic
- salt and pepper

Preparation:
Pile the beans in a saucepan, add water and boil for about 5 minutes, in salted water.

Onion finely chop, you can cut into half rings. Cut the mushrooms into thin slices. A little salt.

In cream or vegetable oil, fry the onions until transparent, add the mushrooms to it, fry for a few minutes until the liquid completely evaporates and the mushrooms begin to be fried.

Add the string beans, finely chopped garlic, salt and pepper to taste. Fry another couple of minutes.

Broccoli with walnuts

Ingredients:

- 500 grams of fresh broccoli
- 1/2 cup walnuts
- 1 onion
- 1/2 cup raisins
- 2 tablespoons olive oil
- salt and pepper

Preparation:

To keep the freshness of cabbage and not lose it while preparing its vitamins, I put it on for 3 minutes at full capacity in a microwave (always covered with a lid, so it does not dry out, as microwaves evaporate liquid from food).

Meanwhile, brown the onion in olive oil, until it is transparent for 5 minutes.

Add to the nuts and raisins, lightly fry on low heat, so as not to burn nuts.

Broccoli is divided into inflorescences. Add it to the onions and nuts.

Mix well. Add salt and pepper to taste.

Made in the USA
San Bernardino, CA
06 June 2019